My First
BENGALI
(Bangla)
DICTIONARY

English-Bengali (Bangla)

Designed and edited by Maria Watson
Translated by Moumita Barak

Hippocrene Books, Inc.
New York

My First Bengali (Bangla) Dictionary

English-Bengali (Bangla)

Hippocrene Books, Inc. edition, 2022

For information, address:
HIPPOCRENE BOOKS, INC.
171 Madison Avenue
New York, NY 10016
www.hippocrenebooks.com

ISBN : 978-0-7818-1431-7

First edition, 2018

Published by arrangement with Biblio Bee Publications, an imprint of ibs Books (UK)
56, Langland Crescent, Stanmore HA7 1NG, U.K.

Printed at Everest Press, New Delhi-110 020 (India)

Aa

actor

অভিনেতা   abhineta

actress

অভিনেত্রী   abhinetri

adult

প্রাপ্তবয়স্ক
praptoboyosko

aeroplane
US English **airplane**

বিমান   biman

air conditioner

শীততাপ নিয়ন্ত্রক যন্ত্র
shitotap niyantrak jantra

air hostess
US English **flight attendant**

বিমানসেবিকা
bimansebika

airport

বিমানবন্দর
bimanbandar

album

এ্যালবাম   ayalbam

almond

বাদাম   badam

alphabet

বর্ণমালা   barnamala

ambulance

এ্যাম্বুলেস   ambulance

angel

ভগবানের দূত
bhagabaner dut

animal

পশু poshu

ankle

গোড়ালি gorali

ant

পিপীলিকা pipilika

antelope

হরিণ বিশেষ
harin bishes

antenna

শুঙ্গ sunga

apartment

কামরা kamra

ape

বাঁদর bandor

apple

আপেল apel

apricot

খুবানি khubani

apron

পরিচ্ছদ-রক্ষক বহিরাবরণ
parichchod-rakshok bohirabaron

aquarium

এ্যাকোয়ারিয়াম
ayakoyariyam

archery

ধনুর্বিদ্যা   dhanurbidya

architect

স্হপতি   sthapati

arm

বাহু   baahu

armour
US English **armor**

বর্ম   bormo

arrow

তীর   teer

artist

শিল্পী   shilpi

asparagus

শতমূলী   shatamuli

astronaut

নভশ্চর   nabhoschor

astronomer

গ্রহ-নক্ষত্র বিশারদ
graha-nakshatra bisharad

athlete

ক্রীড়াবিদ   krirabid

atlas

মানচিত্রাবলী
manachitrabali

aunt

কাকী   kaki

a b c d e f g h i j k l m n o p q r s t u v w x y z

a b c d e f g h i j k l m n o p q r s t u v w x y z

author

লেখক   lekhok

automobile

মোটরগাড়ি   motorgari

autumn

শরৎ   sarat

avalanche

তুষার-ধ্বস   tusar-dhwas

award

পুরস্কার   puroskar

axe

কুঠার   kuthar

baby

বাচ্চা   bachcha

back

পিছনে   pichone

bacon

বেকন   bekon

badge

তকমা   tokma

badminton

ব্যাডমিন্টন খেলা
byadminton khela

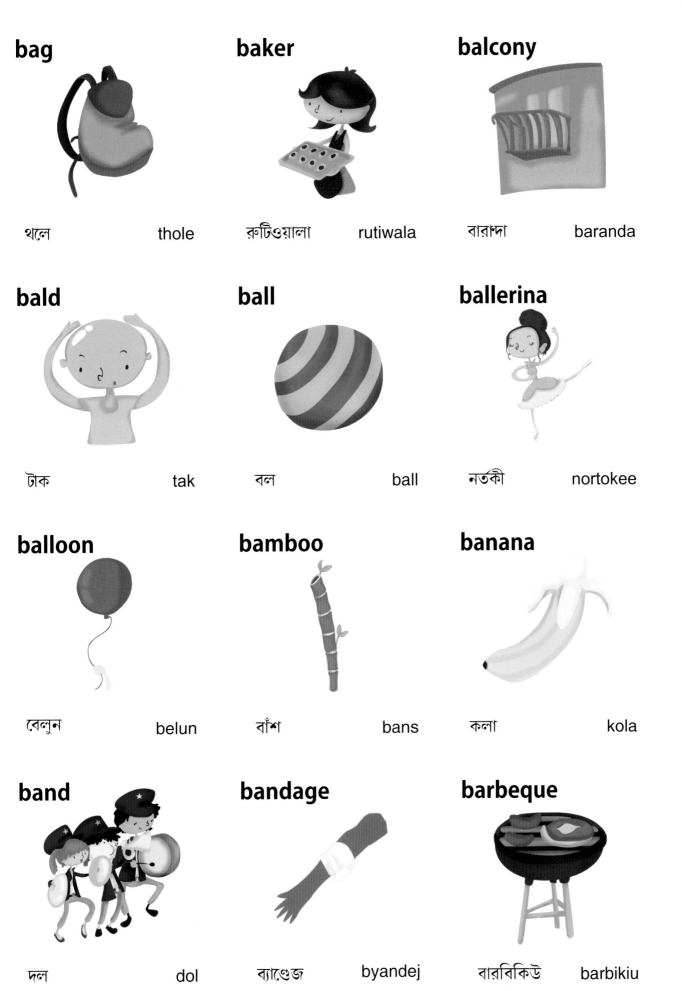

bag

থলে   thole

baker

রুটিওয়ালা   rutiwala

balcony

বারান্দা   baranda

bald

টাক   tak

ball

বল   ball

ballerina

নর্তকী   nortokee

balloon

বেলুন   belun

bamboo

বাঁশ   bans

banana

কলা   kola

band

দল   dol

bandage

ব্যান্ডেজ   byandej

barbeque

বারবিকিউ   barbikiu

barn

শয্যাগার   sasyagar

barrel

পিপা   pipa

baseball

আমেরিকা যুক্তরাষ্ট্রের জাতীয় খেলা
amerika juktarastrer jatiyo khela

basket

ঝুড়ি   jhuri

basketball

বাস্কেটবল   basketbol

bat

বাদুড়   badur

bath

স্নান   snan

battery

ব্যাটারি   byatari

bay

উপসাগর   upasagar

beach

সৈকত   saikat

beak

ঠোঁট   thonth

bean

শিম   sim

bear

ভাল্লুক   bhaluk

beard

দাড়ি   dari

bed

বিছানা   bichana

bee

মৌমাছি   moumachi

beetle

পোকা   poka

beetroot

বীট   beet

bell

ঘটা   ghonta

belt

বেল্ট   belt

berry

বেরি   beri

bicycle

সাইকেল   saikel

billiards
US English **pool**

বিলিয়ার্ড   biliyard

bin

বিন   bin

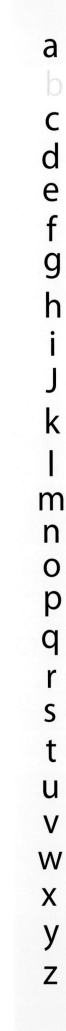

a b c d e f g h i J k l m n o p q r s t u v w x y z

bird

পাখী   pakhee

biscuit

বিস্কুট   biskut

black

কালো   kalo

blackboard

বিদ্যালয়ে লিপির জন্য তক্তা
bidyalaye lipir janya takta

blanket

কম্বল   kambal

blizzard

প্রবল তুষারঝাড়
probol tusharjhar

blood

রক্ত   rokto

blue

নীল   neel

boat

নৌকা   nouka

body

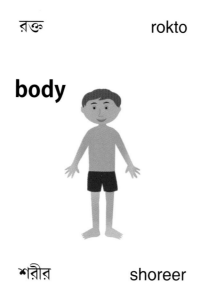

শরীর   shoreer

bone

হাড়   har

book

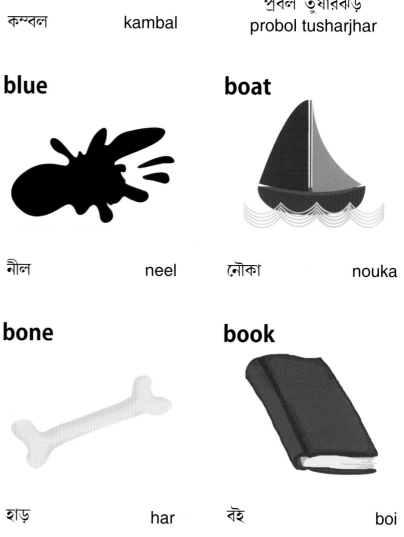

বই   boi

boot

বুট   but

bottle

বোতল   botol

bow

বো টাই   bo tai

bowl

বাটি   bati

box

বাক্স   baksa

boy

বালক   balok

bracelet

ব্রেসলেট   breslet

brain

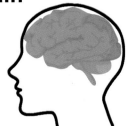

মস্তিষ্ক   mostisko

branch

শাখা   shakha

bread

রুটি   ruti

breakfast

প্রাতঃরাশ   pratorash

brick

ইট   int

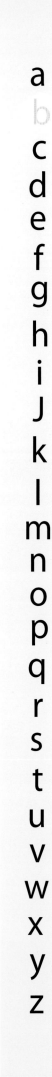

a b c d e f g h i J k l m n o p q r s t u v w x y z

11

bride

নববধূ   nobobodhu

bridegroom

বর   bor

bridge

সেতু   setu

broom

ঝাড়ু   jharu

brother

ভাই   bhai

brown

বাদামী   badami

brush

ব্রাশ   brash

bubble

বুদবুদ   budbud

bucket

বালতি   balti

buffalo

মহিষ   mohish

building

ভবন   bhobon

bulb

বাল্ব   bulb

bull

যাঁড় shnar

bun

বান ban

bunch

গুচ্ছ guchcho

bundle

পাঁজা panja

bungalow

কুঠী kuthi

burger

বার্গার barger

bus

বাস bas

bush

ঝোপ jhop

butcher

কষাই koshai

butter

মাখন makhan

butterfly

প্রজাপতি projapati

button

বোতাম botam

a

c
d
e
f
g
h
i
J
k
l
m
n
o
p
q
r
s
t
u
v
w
x
y
z

Cc

cabbage

বাঁধাকপি bandhakopi

cabinet
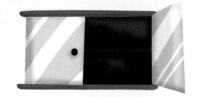
ঢাকা দেওয়া তাক
dhaka dea tak

cable

তার tar

cable car

কেবল কার kebol kar

cactus

ফনিমনসা phonimonsa

cafe

কাফে kafe

cage

খাঁচা khancha

cake

কেক kek

calculator

হিসাবকারী hisabkari

calendar

ক্যালেন্ডর kyalendar

calf

বাছুর bachur

y
z

camel
উট   utt

camera
ক্যামেরা   kyamera

camp
শিবির   shibir

can
ক্যান   kyan

canal
খাল   khal

candle
মোমবাতি   mombati

canoe
ছোট নৌকা
chhoto nouka

canteen
ক্যান্টিন   kyantin

cap
টুপি   tupi

captain
অধিনায়ক   adhinayak

car
গাড়ী   gari

caravan
ভ্যান   bhyan

card

কার্ড   kard

carnival

ভ্রাম্যমাণ আনন্দমেলা
bhrammoman anandmela

carpenter

সূত্রধর   sutradhar

carpet

কার্পেট   karpet

carrot

গাজর   gajor

cart

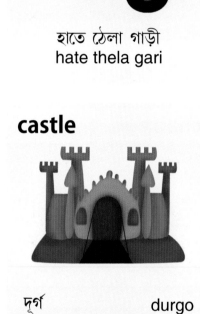

হাতে ঠেলা গাড়ী
hate thela gari

cartoon

কার্টুন   kartun

cascade

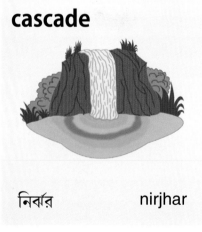

নির্ঝর   nirjhar

castle

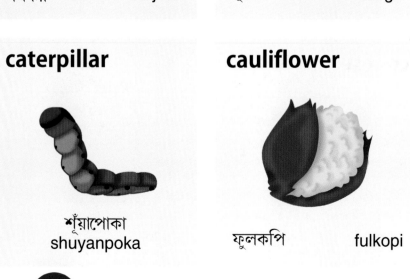

দুর্গ   durgo

cat

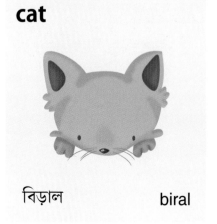

বিড়াল   biral

caterpillar

শুঁয়াপোকা
shuyanpoka

cauliflower

ফুলকপি   fulkopi

cave

গুহা   guha

ceiling

ছাদ   chhad

centipede

শতপদী   satapdi

centre
US English **center**

কেন্দ্র   kendro

cereal

খাদ্যশস্য
khadyosashya

chain

চেন   chen

chair

চেয়ার   cheyar

chalk

খড়ি   khori

cheek

গাল   gal

cheese

পনীর   poneer

chef

রাঁধুনী   randhuni

cherry

চেরি   cheri

chess
দাবা daba

chest
বুক buk

chick
ছানা chhana

chilli
US English **chili**
লঙ্কা lonka

chimney
চিমনি chimni

chin
থুতনি thutni

chocolate
চকোলেট chokolet

christmas
বড়দিনের পর্ব
borodiner porbo

church
গীর্জা geerja

cinema
সিনেমা sinema

circle
বৃত্ত britto

circus
সার্কাস sarkas

city

শহর   sahar

classroom

শ্রেণী কক্ষ
shrenee kakhya

clinic

ক্লিনিক   klinik

clock

ঘড়ি   ghori

cloth

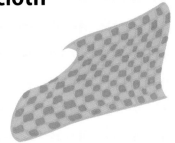

কাপড়   kapor

cloud

মেঘ   megh

clown

জোকার   jokar

coal

কয়লা   koila

coast

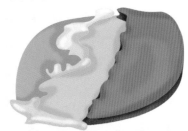

উপকূল   upokul

coat

কোট   kot

cobra

গোখরো সাপ
gokhro sap

cockerel
US English **rooster**

মোরগ   morog

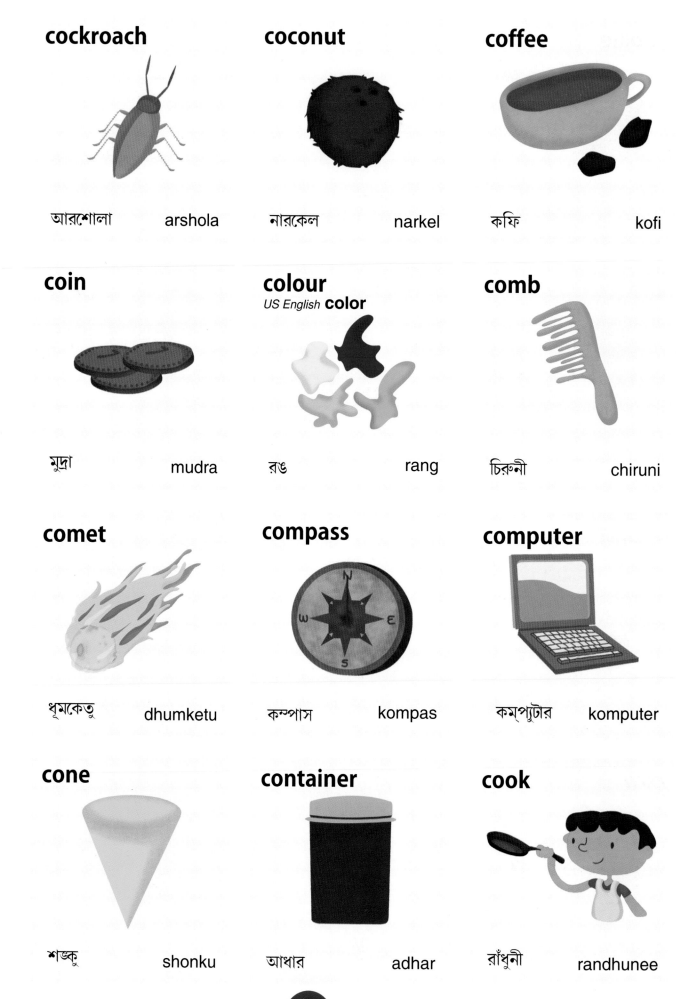

cockroach

আরশোলা   arshola

coconut

নারকেল   narkel

coffee

কফি   kofi

coin

মুদ্রা   mudra

colour
US English **color**

রঙ   rang

comb

চিরুনী   chiruni

comet

ধূমকেতু   dhumketu

compass

কম্পাস   kompas

computer

কম্প্যুটার   komputer

cone

শঙ্কু   shonku

container

আধার   adhar

cook

রাঁধুনী   randhunee

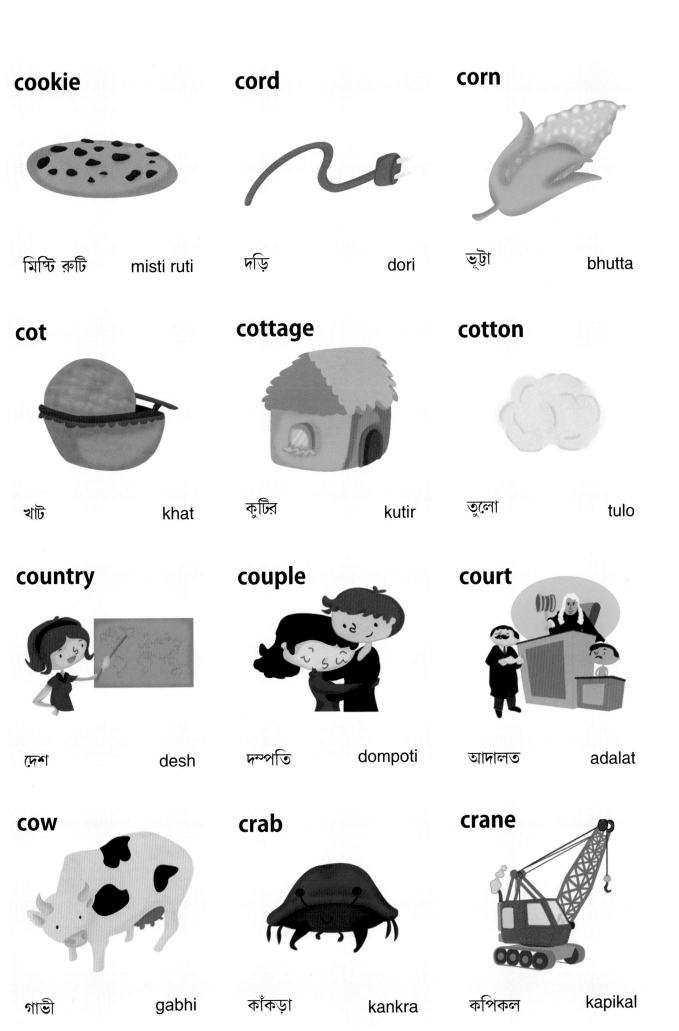

cookie

মিষ্টি রুটি misti ruti

cord

দড়ি dori

corn

ভূট্টা bhutta

cot

খাট khat

cottage

কুটির kutir

cotton

তুলো tulo

country

দেশ desh

couple

দম্পতি dompoti

court

আদালত adalat

cow

গাভী gabhi

crab

কাঁকড়া kankra

crane

কপিকল kapikal

crayon

রঙ্গীন খড়ি
rangeen khori

crocodile

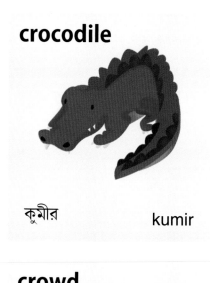

কুমীর
kumir

cross

ত্রুশ
krush

crow

কাক
kak

crowd

ভীড়
bheer

crown

মুকুট
mukut

cube

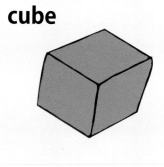

ঘনক্ষেত্র
ghonokhetra

cucumber

শশা
shosha

cup

কাপ
kap

cupboard

আলমারী
almaree

curtain

পর্দা
porda

cushion

গদী
godee

Dd

dam
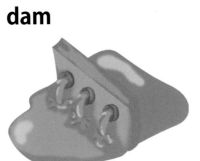
বাঁধ   bandh

dancer

নর্তকী   nartakī

dart

বাণ   baan

data
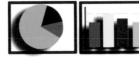
উপাত্ত   upatta

dates

তারিখ   tarikh

daughter

কন্যা   kanya

day

দিন   din

deck

ডেক   dek

deer

হরিণ   harin

den

গর্ত   garta

dentist

দাঁতের ডাক্তার
danter daktar

a b c **d** e f g h i J k l m n o p q r s t u v w x y z

desert

মরুভূমি marubhumi

design

নকশা naksha

desk

ডেস্ক desk

dessert

ডেজার্ট dejert

detective

গোয়েন্দা goyenda

diamond

হীরা heera

diary

দিনলিপি dinlipi

dice

পাশা pasha

dictionary

অভিধান abhidhan

dinosaur

অধুনালুপ্ত সরীসৃপ বিশেষ
adhunalupta sarisrip bishes

disc

ডিস্ক disk

dish

থালা thala

diver

ডুবুরী   duburee

dock

কদর   bandar

doctor

ডাক্তার   daktar

dog

কুকুর   kukur

doll

পুতুল   putul

dolphin

শুশুক   shushuk

dome

গম্বুজ   gambuj

domino

পৌর ক্রীড়াবিশেষ
paura krirabishes

donkey

গাধা   gadha

donut

ডোনাট   donut

door

দরজা   darja

dough

মাখা ময়দার তাল
makha moidar tal

a b c e f g h i j k l m n o p q r s t u v w x y z

a b c d e f g h i j k l m n o p q r s t u v w x y z

dragon

ঘুড়ি বিশেষ
ghuri bishes

drain

নর্দমা nardama

drawer

টানা tana

drawing

অঙ্কন ankan

dream

স্বপ্ন sapna

dress

পোশাক poshak

drink

পান করা pan kora

driver

চালক chalak

drop

বিন্দু bindu

drought

খরা khara

drum

ঢাক dhak

duck

হাঁস hans

dustbin
US English **trash can**

নোংরা ফেলার জায়গা
nongra pheler jayga

duvet

লেপ   lep

dwarf

বামন   bamon

Ee

eagle

ঈগল   eagle

ear

কান   kan

earring

কানের দুল   kaner dul

earth

পৃথিবী   prithibi

earthquake

ভূমিকম্প
bhumikampa

earthworm

কেঁচো   kencho

eclipse

গ্রহণ   grahan

edge

প্রান্ত   pranta

a b c d e f g h i j k l m n o p q r s t u v w x y z

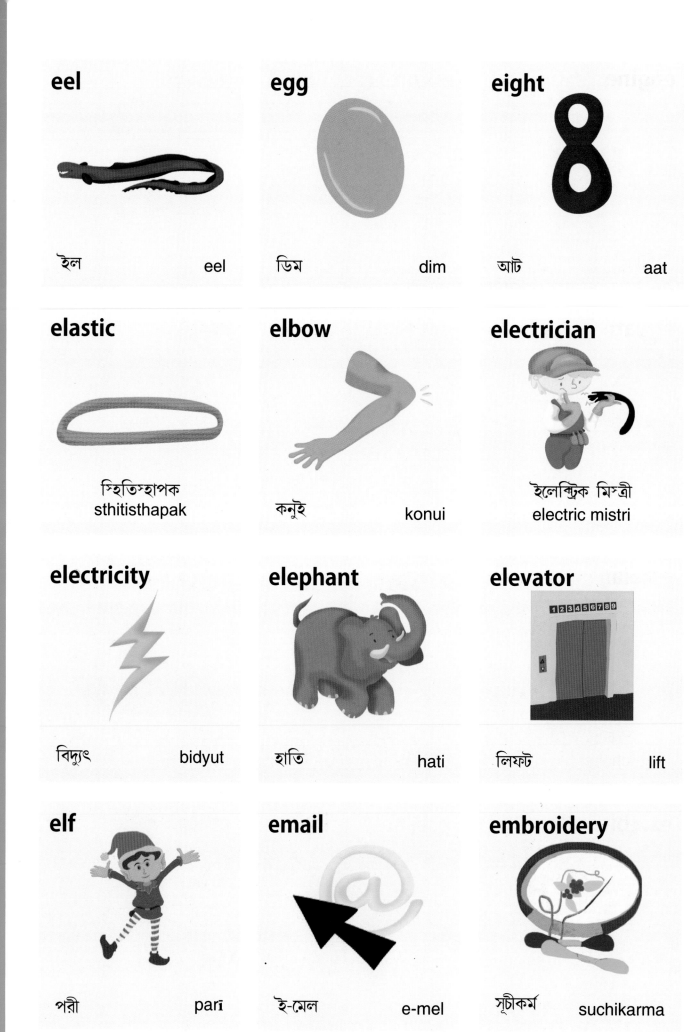

eel

ইল eel

egg

ডিম dim

eight

আট aat

elastic

স্হিতিস্হাপক
sthitisthapak

elbow

কনুই konui

electrician

ইলেক্ট্রিক মিস্ত্রী
electric mistri

electricity

বিদ্যুৎ bidyut

elephant

হাতি hati

elevator

লিফট lift

elf

পরী pari

email

ই-মেল e-mel

embroidery

সূচীকর্ম suchikarma

abcdefghiJklmnopqrstuvwxyz

engine

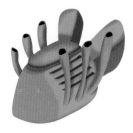

ইঞ্জিন   injin

entrance

প্রবেশদ্বার   prabeshdar

envelope

খাম   kham

equator

নিরক্ষরেখা
niraksarekha

equipment

যন্ত্রপাতি   jantrapati

eraser

রবার   rabar

escalator

চলন্ত সিঁড়ি
chalanta sinri

eskimo

এস্কিমো   eskimo

evening

সন্ধ্যা   sandhya

exhibition

প্রদর্শনী   pradarsani

eye

চোখ   chokh

eyebrow

ভ্রু   bhru

a b c d e f g h i j k l m n o p q r s t u v w x y z

a b c d e f g h i j k l m n o p q r s t u v w x y z

Ff

fabric

কাপড় kapor

face

মুখ mukh

factory

কারখানা karkhana

fairy

পরী pari

family

পরিবার paribar

fan

পাখা pakha

farm

খামার khamar

farmer

কৃষক krishok

fat

মোটা mota

father

বাবা baba

feather

পালক palak

female

মহিলা   mahila

fence

বেড়া   bera

ferry

খেয়া   kheya

field

ক্ষেত্র   khetra

fig

ডুমুর   dumur

file

ফাইল   phail

film

চলচ্চিত্র   chalachitra

finger

আঙুল   angul

fire

আগুন   agun

fire engine

দমকল   damakal

fire fighter

দমকল কর্মী
damkal karmi

fireworks

বাজি   baji

a b c d e f g h i j k l m n o p q r s t u v w x y z

fish

মাছ — maach

fist

মুষ্টি — musti

five

পাঁচ — panch

flag

পতাকা — pataka

flame

শিখা — sikha

flamingo

মরাল — marral

flask

ফ্লাস্ক — phlask

flock

পাল — pal

flood

বন্যা — banya

floor

মেঝে — mejhe

florist

মালী — mali

flour

ময়দা — mayad

flower

ফুল   phul

flute

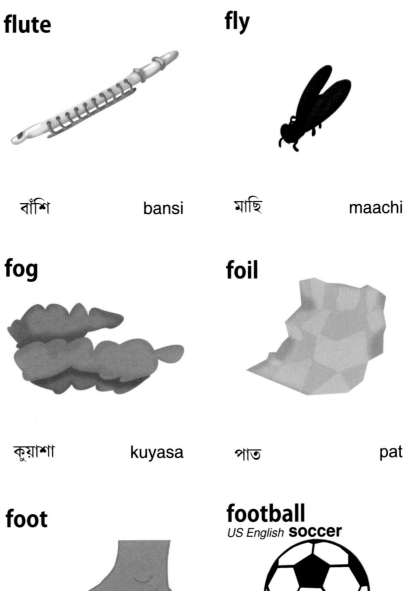

বাঁশি   bansi

fly

মাছি   maachi

foam

ফেনা   phena

fog

কুয়াশা   kuyasa

foil

পাত   pat

food

খাদ্য   khadya

foot

পা   paa

football

US English **soccer**

ফুটবল   phutbal

forearm

বাহু   bahu

forehead

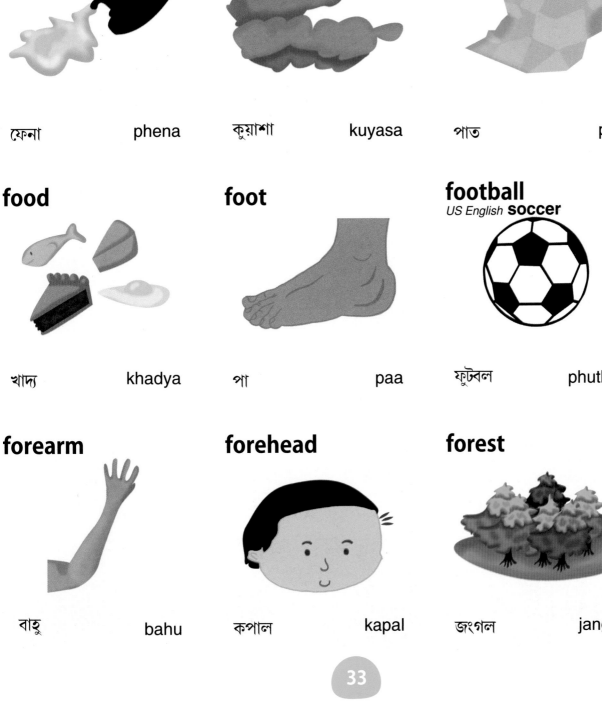

কপাল   kapal

forest

জংগল   jangal

a b c d e **f** g h i j k l m n o p q r s t u v w x y z

a
b
c
d
e
f
g
h
i
j
J
k
l
m
n
o
p
q
r
s
t
u
v
w
x
y
z

fork

কাটা-চামচ
kanta-chamuch

fortress

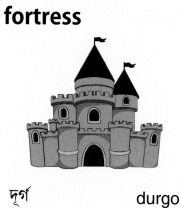

দুর্গ durgo

fountain

ফোয়ারা phoyara

four

চার char

fox

শিয়াল shiyal

frame

ফ্রেম phrem

freezer

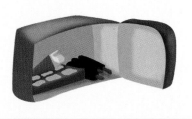

হিমায়ক himayak

fridge
US English **refrigerator**

রেফ্রিজারেটর
rephrijaretar

friend

বন্ধু bandhu

frog

ব্যাঙ beng

fruit

ফল phal

fumes

ধোঁয়া dhonya

funnel

ফানেল   phānel

furnace

অগ্নিকুণ্ড   agnikuṇḍa

furniture

আসবাবপত্র
asbabpatra

Gg

gadget

গ্যাজেট   gyajet

gallery

দর-দালান   dar-dalan

game

খেলা   khela

gap

ফাঁক   phank

garage

গ্যারেজ   gyarej

garbage

আবর্জনা   abarjana

garden

বাগান   bagan

garland

মালা   mala

a b c d e f g h i J k l m n o p q r s t u v w x y z

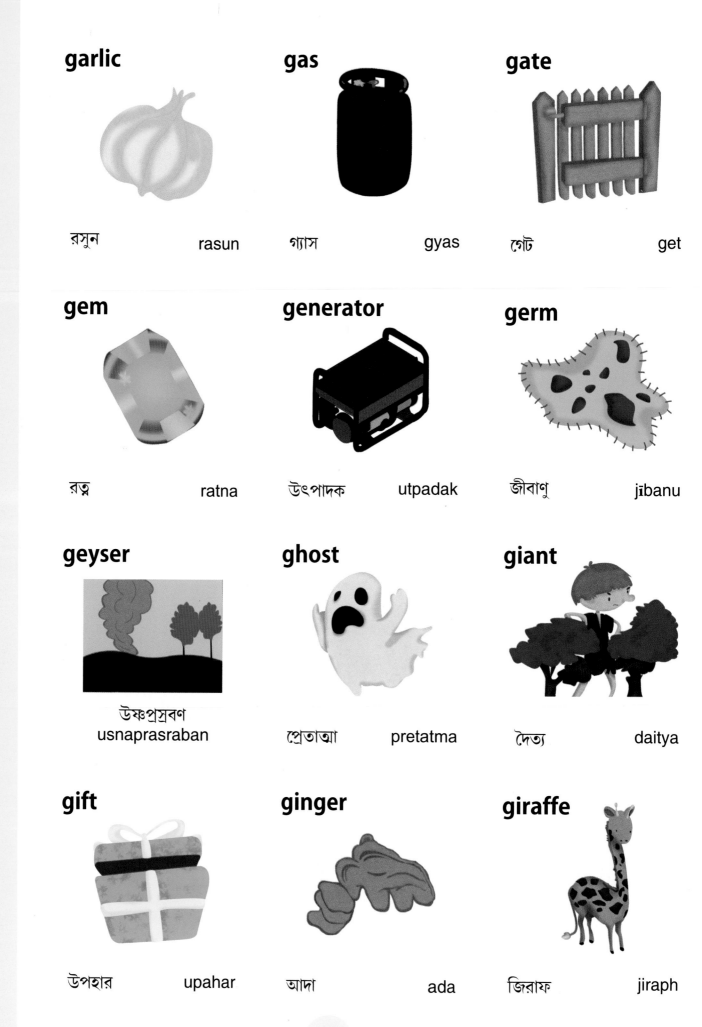

garlic

রসুন   rasun

gas

গ্যাস   gyas

gate

গেট   get

gem

রত্ন   ratna

generator

উৎপাদক   utpadak

germ

জীবাণু   jibanu

geyser

উষ্ণপ্রস্রবণ
usnaprasraban

ghost

প্রেতাত্মা   pretatma

giant

দৈত্য   daitya

gift

উপহার   upahar

ginger

আদা   ada

giraffe

জিরাফ   jiraph

girl

মেয়ে   meye

glacier

হিমবাহ   himabaha

glass

কাঁচ   kanch

glider

ইঞ্জিনহীন বিমান
Inginehin biman

globe

পৃথিবী   prithibi

glove

দস্তানা   dastana

glue

আঠা   atha

goal

লক্ষ্য   lakhsya

goat

ছাগল   chagol

gold

স্বর্ণ   sarnaa

golf

গলফ   golf

goose

রাজহংসী   rajahansi

a b c d e f g h i J k l m n o p q r s t u v w x y z

gorilla

বনমানুষ
banmanush

grain

শস্য   sasya

grandfather

পিতামহ   pitamaha

grandmother

দিদা   dida

grape

আঙুর   angur

grapefruit

জাম্বুরা   jambura

grass

ঘাস   ghas

grasshopper

ফড়িং   pharing

gravel
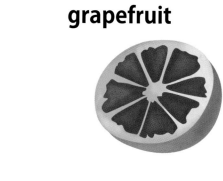
নুড়ি   nuri

green

সবুজ   sabuj

grey
ধূসর   dhusar

grill

স্যাঁকা   sanka

grocery

মুদিখানা   mudikhana

ground

মাঠ   math

guard

পাহারা   pahara

guava

পেয়ারা   peyara

guide

প্রদর্শক   pradarshak

guitar

গীটার   gitar

gulf

উপসাগর   upasagar

gun

বন্দুক   banduk

gypsy

যাযাবর   jajabar

Hh

hair

চুল   chul

hairbrush

চুলের ব্রাশ
chuler brush

a b c d e f g h i J k l m n o p q r s t u v w x y z

hairdresser

নাপিত   napit

half

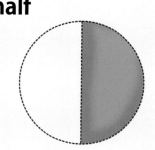

অর্ধেক   ardhek

hall

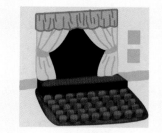

হল   hal

ham

হ্যাম   hyam

hammer

হাতুড়ি   haturi

hammock

বিছানা বিশেষ
bichana bishes

hand

হাত   hat

handbag

হাতব্যাগ   hathbag

handicraft

হাতের কাজ   hater kaj

handkerchief

রুমাল   rumal

handle

হাতল   hatal

hanger

হ্যাঙ্গার   hangar

harbour
US English **harbor**

কদর   bandar

hare

খরগোশ   khargos

harvest

ফসল   phasal

hat

টুপী   tupi

hawk

বাজপাখী   bajpakhii

hay

খড়   khar

head

মাথা   matha

headphone

কানে লাগাইয়া ধ্বনি শোনার যন্ত্র
kane lagaiya dhwani sonar jantra

heap

গাদা   gada

heart

হৃদয়   hriday

heater

উনুন   unun

hedge

ঝোপের বেড়া
jhoper bera

heel
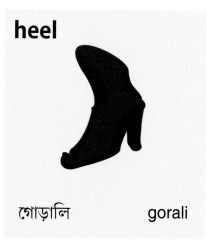
গোড়ালি　gorali

helicopter

হেলিকপ্টার　helikopter

helmet

শিরস্ত্রাণ　sirastran

hen

মুর্গী　murgi

herb

ঔষধি　ausadhi

herd

পশুপাল　pasupal

hermit

সাধু　sadhu

hill

পাহাড়　pahar

hippopotamus
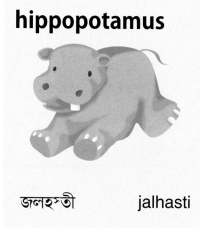
জলহস্তী　jalhasti

hive
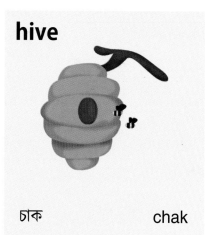
চাক　chak

hole
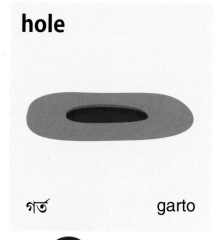
গর্ত　garto

honey
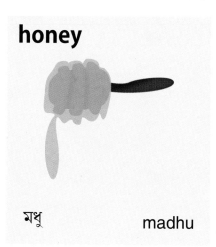
মধু　madhu

hood

ঘোমটা   ghomta

hook

হুক   huk

horn

শিঙ   shing

horse

ঘোড়া   ghora

hose
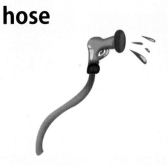

জলের পাইপ
jaler pipe

hospital

হাসপাতাল   haspatal

hotdog

হট-ডগ   hot-dog

hotel

হোটেল   hotel

hour

ঘণ্টা   ghanṭa

house

ঘর   ghar

human

মানব   manab

hunter

শিকারী   sikari

hurricane

হ্যারিকেন hyariken

husband

স্বামী shami

hut

কুটির kuṭir

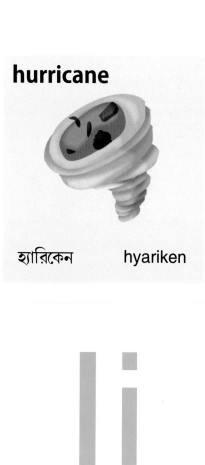

ice

বরফ baraph

iceberg

হিমশৈল himshaila

ice cream

আইসক্রীম aiskrim

idol

মূর্তি murti

igloo

এস্কিমোসদের কুটির
eskimosder kutir

inch

ইঞ্চি inchi

injection

ইঞ্জেকশন injekshan

injury

আঘাত aghat

ink

কালি   kali

inn

সরাইখানা   saraikhana

insect

পোকা   poka

inspector

পরিদর্শক   paridarsak

instrument

যন্ত্র   yantra

internet

ইন্টারনেট   intaranet

intestine

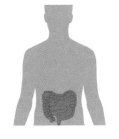

অন্ত্র   antra

inventor

উদ্ভাবক   udbhabak

invitation

আমন্ত্রণ   amantrana

iron

লোহা   loha

island

দ্বীপ   dip

ivory

আইভরি   aibhari

a b c d e f g h **i** j k l m n o p q r s t u v w x y z

a b c d e f g h i **J** k l m n o p q r s t u v w x y z

Jj

jackal

শৃগাল   srigal

jacket

জ্যাকেট   jyaket

jackfruit

কাঁঠাল   kathal

jam
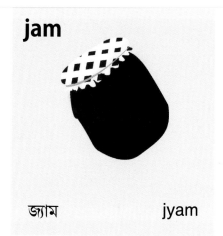
জ্যাম   jyam

jar
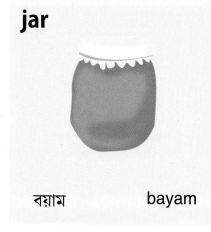
বয়াম   bayam

javelin

বর্শা   barsa

jaw
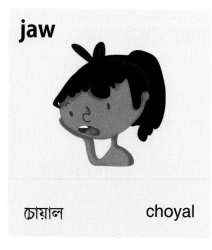
চোয়াল   choyal

jeans

জিন্স   jins

jelly

জেলি   jeli

jetty

জেটি   jeti

jewellery
US English **jewelry**
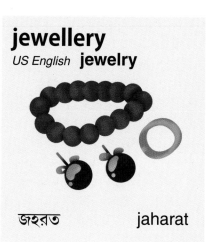
জহরত   jaharat

jigsaw

জিগস   jigasa

jockey

জকি   jaki

joker

ভাঁড়   bhamr

journey

যাত্রা   yatra

jug

জলপাত্র   jalapatra

juggler

বাজিকর   bajikar

juice

রস   ras

jungle

জঙ্গল   jangal

jute

পাট   pat

Kk

kangaroo

ক্যাঙ্গারু   kyangaru

kennel

কুঁড়ে ঘর   kuure ghar

kerb
US English **curb**

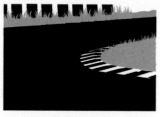

প্রতিবন্ধক
pratibandhak

kerosene

কেরোসিন তেল
kerosin tel

ketchup

কেচ্ আপ kech aap

kettle

কেটলি ketli

key

চাবি chabi

keyboard

কীবোর্ড kiborde

key ring

চাবির রিং chabir ring

kidney

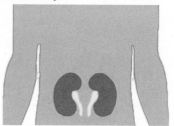

বৃক্ক brikka

kilogram

কিলোগ্রাম kilogram

king

রাজা raja

kiosk

ক্ষুদ্র দোকান
khudra dokan

kiss

চুম্বন cumban

kitchen

রান্নাঘর   rannaghar

kite

ঘুড়ি   ghuṛi

kitten

বিড়াল ছানা
biral chana

kiwi

এক ধরনের ফল
ek dharaner fal

knee

হাঁটু   hantu

knife

ছুরি   churi

knight

রক্ষক ঘোড়সওয়ারী
rakhak ghorsaoari

knitwear

উল দিয়ে তৈরী বস্ত্র
ul diye tayri bastra

knob

হাতল   hatal

knock

টোকা   toka

knot

গিঁট   gint

knuckle

মুঠোর গাঁট
muthor gant

Ll

label

এক ধরনের ট্যাগ
ek dharner tag

laboratory

পরীক্ষাগার   parikhagar

lace

জরি   jari

ladder

মই   mai

lady

ভদ্রমহিলা
bhadramahila

ladybird
US English **ladybug**

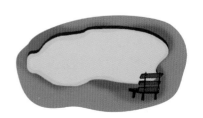

এক ধরনের পোকা
ek dharaner poka

lagoon

উপহ্রদ   upahrad

lake

হ্রদ   hrad

lamb

মেষ শাবক   mesh sabak

lamp

বাতি   bati

lamp post

বাতি পোস্ট   bati post

land

জমি jami

lane

গলি gali

lantern

লণ্ঠন lanthan

laser

শক্তিশালী লাইট
shaktishali lite

lasso

ফাঁস-দড়ি phash dari

latch

হুড়কা hurka

laundry

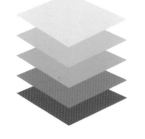

লণ্ড্রি landri

lawn

বনভূমি banbhumi

lawyer

আইনজীবী ainjibi

layer

স্তর stor

leaf

পাতা pata

leather

চামড়া chamra

a b c d e f g h i J k l m n o p q r s t u v w x y z

leg

পা   pa

lemon

লেবু   lebu

lemonade

লেবুর শরবত
lebur sarbat

lens

লেন্স   lens

leopard

চিতা   chita

letter

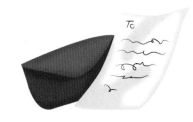

চিঠি   chithi

letterbox
US English **mailbox**

লেটারবক্স   leter baksh

lettuce

স্যালাদ   salad

library

গ্রহাগার   granthagar

licence

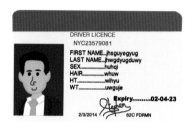

লাইসেন্স   laisens

lid

ঢাকনা   dhakna

light

আলো   alo

52

lighthouse

বাতিঘর   batighar

limb

ডানা   dana

line

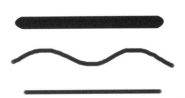

লাইন   line

lion

সিংহ   sinha

lip

ঠোঁট   thoth

lipstick

লিপস্টিক   lipastik

liquid

তরল   taral

list

তালিকা   talika

litre

US English **liter**

লিটার   litar

living room

বসার ঘর   basar ghar

lizard

টিকটিকি   tiktiki

load

বোঝা   bojha

a b c d e f g h i J k l m n o p q r s t u v w x y z

a
b
c
d
e
f
g
h
i
J
k
l
m
n
o
p
q
r
s
t
u
v
w
x
y
z

loaf

ডেলা dela

lobster

গলদা চিংড়ি
galada chingri

lock

তালা tala

loft

চিলেকোঠা chilekothe

log

কাঠের গুঁড়ি
kather gunri

loop

লুপ lup

lorry
US English **truck**

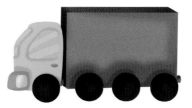

লরি বাহন lari bahaon

lotus

পদ্ম padma

louse

উকুন ukun

luggage

লটবহর latbahar

lunch

লাঞ্চ lanch

lung

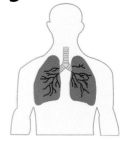

ফুসফুস phusaphus

Mm

machine

মেশিন   mesin

magazine

পত্রিকা   patrika

magician

জাদুকর   jadukar

magnet

চুম্বক   chumbak

magpie

বাচাল   bachal

mail

মেইল   meail

mammal

স্তন্যপায়ী প্রাণী
stanapay prani

man

মানুষ   manus

mandolin

ম্যান্ডোলীন   myandolin

mango
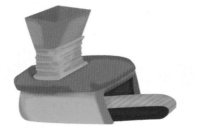
আম   aam

map
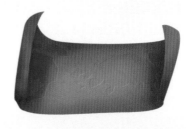
মানচিত্র   manchitra

maple

পাতাবিশেষ patabises

marble

মার্বেল marbel

market

বাজার bajar

mask

মুখোশ mukhosh

mast

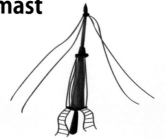

মাস্তুল mastul

mat

মাদুর madur

matchbox

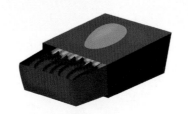

দেশলাই বাক্স
deslai bakeso

mattress

গদি gadi

meal

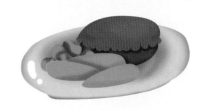

খাবার khabar

meat

মাংস manso

mechanic

মিস্ত্রী mistri

medicine

ওষধ ausadh

melon

তরমুজ taramuj

merchant

বণিক banik

mermaid

মৎসকন্যা matsakanya

metal

ধাতু dhatu

metre
US English **meter**

মিটার mitar

microphone

মাইক maike

microwave

মাইক্রোওয়েভ
maikrowave

mile

মাইল maile

milk

দুধ dudh

miner

খনিজীবী khanijibi

mineral

খনিজ khanij

mint

পুদিনা pudina

minute

মিনিট   minit

mirror

আয়না   ayna

mobile phone

মোবাইল ফোন
mobile phone

model

মডেল   madel

mole

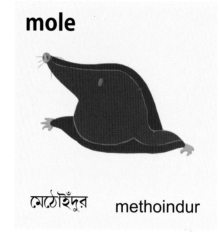

মেঠোইঁদুর   methoindur

money

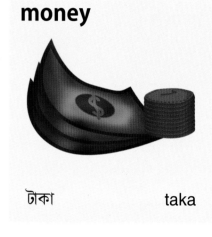

টাকা   taka

monk

সন্ন্যাসী   sannyasi

monkey

বানর   banar

monster

দৈত্য   daitya

month

মাস   mas

monument

স্মৃতি স্তম্ভ
smriti stambha

moon

চাঁদ   chand

mop

পেঁচা pancha

morning

সকাল sakal

mosquito

মশা masa

moth

পোকা poka

mother

মা ma

motorcycle

মোটর সাইকেল
motarsaikel

motorway

রাস্তার ধারের
rastar dharer

mountain

পর্বত parbat

mouse

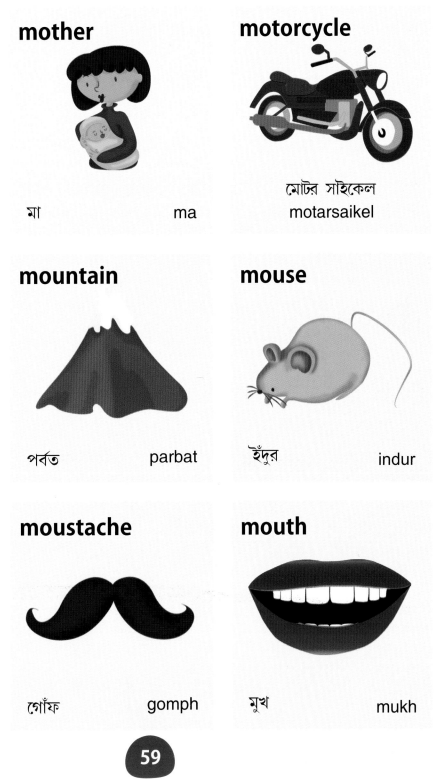

ইঁদুর indur

mousetrap

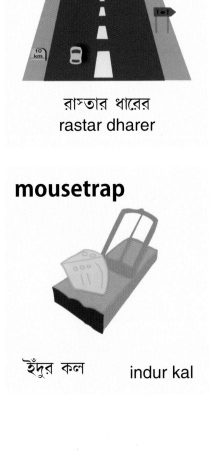

ইঁদুর কল indur kal

moustache

গোঁফ gomph

mouth

মুখ mukh

mud

কাদা   kada

muffin

মাফিন   maphin

mug

মগ   mag

mule

খচ্চর   khachar

muscle
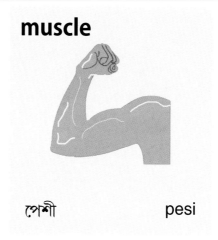
পেশী   pesi

museum

জাদুঘর   jadughar

mushroom

মাশরুম   mashrum

music

সঙ্গীত   sangit

musician

সুরকার   surakar

Nn

nail

পেরেক   perek

napkin

ন্যাপকিন   nyapkin

nappy
US English **diaper**

ন্যাপি · nappy

nature

প্রকৃতি · prakriti

neck

ঘাড় · ghar

necklace

নেকলেস · nekles

necktie

নেকটাই · nektai

needle

ছুঁচ · chuch

neighbour
US English **neighbor**

প্রতিবেশী · pratibesi

nest

নীড় · nir

net

জাল · jal

newspaper

সংবাদপত্র
sambadpatra

night

রাত · rat

nine

নয় · naya

a b c d e f g h i j k l **m** n o p q r s t u v w x y z

noodles

নুডল্স   nudals

noon

দুপুর   dupur

north

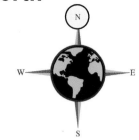

উত্তর   uttar

nose

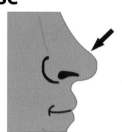

নাক   nak

note

চিরকুট   chirkut

notebook

নোট বই   not bai

notice

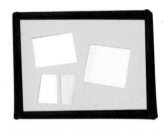

বিজ্ঞপ্তি   bigyapti

number

সংখ্যা   sankhya

nun

মঠবাসিনী   mathabasini

nurse

নার্স   nars

nursery

শিশুশালা   sisusala

nut

বাদাম   badam

Oo

oar

বৈঠা   baitha

observatory

মানমন্দির
manmandir

ocean
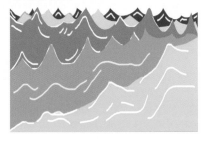
মহাসাগর   mahasagar

octopus

অক্টোপাস   aktopas

office

দপ্তর   daptar

oil

তেল   tel

olive

জলপাই   jalpai

omelette
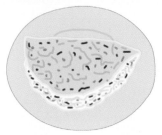
অমলেট   amalet

one

এক   ek

onion

পেঁয়াজ   penyaj

orange

কমলা   kamala

a b c d e f g h i j k l m n o p q r s t u v w x y z

orbit

অক্ষিকোটর
akhikotar

orchard

ফলের বাগান
phaler bagan

orchestra

অর্কেস্ট্রা
arkestra

ostrich

উট পাখী
ut pakhi

otter

ভোঁদড়
bhomdar

oval

উপ-বৃত্তাকার
up-brittakar

oven

উনুন
unun

owl

পেঁচা
pemcha

ox

বলদ
balad

Pp

packet

মোড়ক
morak

page

পৃষ্ঠা
prishtha

pain
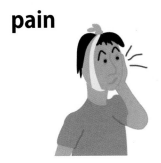
ব্যথা — byatha

paint

রং — rangh

painting

চিত্র — citra

pair

যুগল — yugal

palace
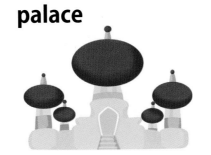
প্রাসাদ — prasad

palm

করতল — karatal

pan

চাটু — chatu

pancake

প্যানকেক — pyanakek

panda

পাণ্ডা — panda

papaya

পেঁপে — pempe

paper

কাগজ — kagoj

parachute
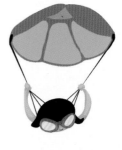
প্যারাশুট — pyarasut

parcel

মোড়ক   morak

park

পার্ক   park

parrot

টিয়া পাখী   tiya pakhi

passenger

যাত্রী   yatri

pasta

পাস্তা   pasta

pastry

প্যাস্ট্রী   pastri

pavement

ফুটপাথ   phutpath

paw

থাবা   thaba

pea

মটর   matar

peach

পীচ   pīch

peacock

ময়ুর   mayur

peak

শিখর   sikhar

peanut

চিনাবাদাম   chinabadam

pear

নাশপাতি   naspati

pearl

মুক্তা   mukta

pedal

প্যাডেল   pyadel

pelican

পেলিকান   pelikyan

pen

কলম   kalam

pencil

পেন্সিল   pensil

penguin

পেঙ্গুইন   penguin

pepper

গোলমরিচ   golmarich

perfume

সুগন্ধি   sugandhi

pet

পোষা   posa

pharmacy

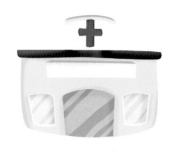

ঔষধালয়   ausadhalaya

a b c d e f g h i j k l m n o **p** q r s t u v w x y z

photograph

আলোকচিত্র
alokchitra

piano

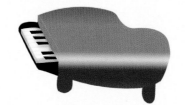

পিয়ানো   piyano

picture

ছবি   chabi

pie

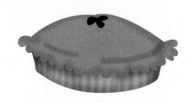

পাই   pai

pig

শূকর   sukar

pigeon

পায়রা   payra

pillar

স্তম্ভ   stambh

pillow

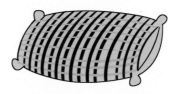

বালিশ   balis

pilot

চালক   chalak

pineapple

আনারস   anaras

pink

গোলাপী রং
golapi rong

pipe

নল   nal

pizza

পিজ্জা   pijja

planet

গ্রহ   graha

plant

উদ্ভিদ   udbhid

plate

প্লেট   plet

platform

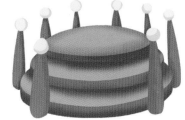

মাচা   macha

platypus

প্লাটিপাস   platipas

player

খেলোয়াড়   kheloyar

plum

ফলবিশেষ   falbisesh

plumber

কলমিস্ত্রী   kalmistri

plywood

কাঠ বিশেষ
kath bisesh

pocket

পকেট   paket

poet

কবি   kabi

polar bear

মেরু ভল্লুক

meru bhaluk

police

পুলিশ

pulis

pollution

দূষণ

dusan

pomegranate

ডালিম

dalim

pond

পুকুর

pukur

porcupine

শজারু

sajaru

port

বন্দর

bandar

porter

কুলি

kuli

postcard

পোস্টকার্ড

postkard

postman

পিয়ন

pion

post office

ডাক ঘর

dak ghor

pot

পাত্র

patre

potato

আলু   alu

powder

গুঁড়া   gura

prawn
US English **shrimp**

চিংড়ি   chingri

priest

পুরোহিত   purohit

prince

রাজপুত্র   rajputra

prison

কারাগার   karagar

pudding

পুডিং   puding

pump

পাম্প   pamp

pumpkin

কুমড়ো   kumro

puppet

পুতুল   putul

puppy

কুকুর ছানা
kukurchana

purse

টাকার থলি   takar thali

quail

কোয়েল   quail

quarry

পাথরের খনি
patharer khani

queen

রাণী   rani

queue

কিউ   kiu

quiver

তূণীর   tunir

Rr

rabbit

খরগোশ   khargos

rack

তাক   tak

racket

র‍্যাকেট   racket

radio

রেডিও   redio

radish

মূলো   mulo

raft

ভেলা   bhela

rain

বৃষ্টি   bristi

rainbow

রামধনু   ramdhanu

raisin

কিশমিশ   kismis

ramp

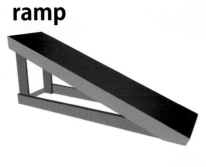

র্যাম্প   ramp

raspberry

ফল বিশেষ
phal bishes

rat

ইঁদুর   indur

razor

ক্ষুর   khur

receipt

প্রাপ্তি   prapti

rectangle

আয়তক্ষেত্র
ayataksetra

red

লাল   lal

restaurant

রেস্টুরেন্ট   resturent

a b c d e f g h i j k l m n o p q **r** s t u v w x y z

rhinoceros

গণ্ডার   gandar

rib

পাঁজর   panjar

ribbon

ফিতা   phita

rice

ধান   dhan

ring

রিং   ring

river

নদী   nadī

road

রাস্তা   rasta

robber

ডাকাত   dakat

robe

পোশাক   poshak

robot

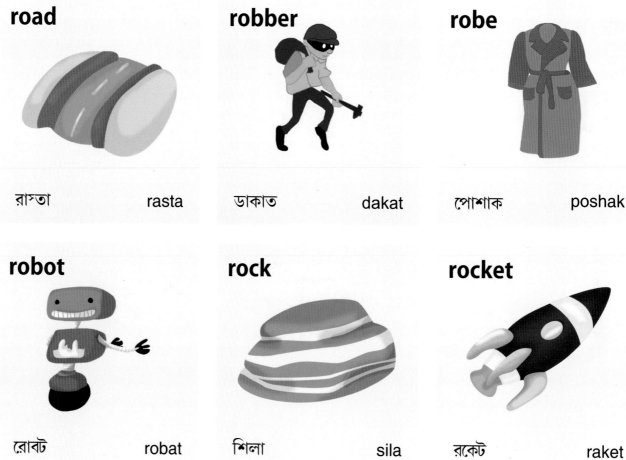

রোবট   robat

rock

শিলা   sila

rocket

রকেট   raket

roller coaster

রোলার কোস্টার
rolar kostar

room

কক্ষ   kakho

root

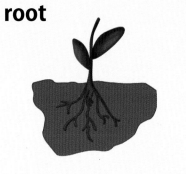

শিকড়   sikar

rope

দড়ি   dari

rose

গোলাপ   golap

round

বৃত্তাকার   brittakar

rug

কম্বল   kambal

rugby

রাগবি খেলা
ragabi khela

ruler

শাসক   sasak

Ss

sack

বস্তা   basta

sail

পাল   pal

a b c d e f g h i j k l m n o p q r s t u v w x y z

sailor

নাবিক nabik

salad

স্যালাদ salad

salt

লবণ laban

sand

বালি bali

sandwich

স্যাণ্ডউইচ syandauich

satellite

উপগ্রহ upagraha

saucer

ছোট থালা choto thala

sausage

সসেজ saseja

saw

করাত karat

scarf

স্কার্ফ skarph

school

স্কুল skul

scissors

কাঁচি kanchi

scooter

স্কুটার   skutar

scorpion

বৃশ্চিক   brischik

screw

স্ক্রু   skru

sea

সমুদ্র   samudra

seal

সীল   sil

seat

আসন   asan

see-saw

দোলনা   dolna

seven

সাত   sat

shadow

ছায়া   chaya

shampoo

শ্যাম্পু   syampu

shark

হাঙ্গর   hangar

sheep

মেষ   mes

shelf

তাক   tak

shell

খোল   khol

shelter

আশ্রয়   asroy

ship

জাহাজ   jahaj

shirt

শার্ট   sart

shoe

জুতা   juta

shorts

হাফ প্যান্ট   haph pyant

shoulder

কাঁধ   kandh

shower

ঝারনা   jharana

shutter

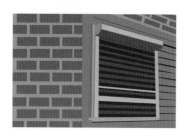

শাটার   shutter

shuttlecock

শ্যাটল কক্   syatal kak

signal

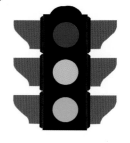

সংকেত   sanket

silver

রূপা   rupa

sink

ডুবা   duba

sister

বোন   bon

six

ছয়   chay

skate

স্কেইট   skeit

skeleton

কঙ্কাল   kanikal

ski

স্কী   ski

skin

চামড়া   camara

skirt

স্কার্ট   skart

skull

খুলি   khuli

sky

আকাশ   akas

skyscraper

গগনচুম্বী
gaganacumbī

a b c d e f g h i j k l m n o p q r s t u v w x y z

slide

স্লাইড   slā'iḍ

slipper

চপ্পল   chappal

smoke

ধোঁওয়া   dhonya

snail

শামুক   samuk

snake

সাপ   sap

snow

তুষার   tushar

soap

সাবান   saban

sock

মোজা   moja

sofa

সোফা   sopha

soil

মাটি   mati

soldier

সৈনিক   sainik

soup

সুপ   sup

space

স্হান   sthan

spaghetti

স্প্যাঘেটি   spyaghati

sphere

গোলক   golak

spider

মাকড়শা   makarsha

spinach

শাক   sak

sponge

স্পঞ্জ   sponge

spoon

চামচ   chamoch

spray

স্প্রে   spre

spring

বসন্ত   basanta

square

বর্গক্ষেত্র
bargakhetra

squirrel

কাঠবিড়ালী   kathbirali

stadium

স্টেডিয়াম   stediyam

a b c d e f g h i j k l m n o p q r s t u v w x y z

stairs

সিঁড়ি

siree

stamp

স্ট্যাম্প

styamp

star

তারকা

taraka

station

স্টেশন

stesan

statue

মূর্তি

murti

stethoscope

স্টেথোস্কোপ

stetheskop

stomach

পেট

pet

stone

পাথর

pathar

storm

ঝড়

jhar

straw

খড়

khar

strawberry

স্ট্রবেরী

straberi

street

রাস্তা

rasta

student

ছাত্র   chatra

submarine

ডুবোজাহাজ   dubojahaj

subway

ভূগর্ভস্থ পথ
bhugarbhastha path

sugar

চিনি   chini

sugarcane

আখ   akh

summer

গ্রীষ্ম   grisma

sun

সূর্য   surya

supermarket

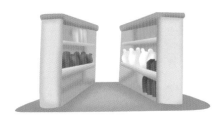

সুপার মার্কেট
supar market

swan

রাজহাঁস   rajahans

sweet

মিষ্টি   misti

swimming pool

সুইমিং পুল   suiming pul

swimsuit

সাঁতারের পোশাক
santarer poshak

swing

দোলনা   dolna

switch

সুইচ   suich

syrup

সিরাপ   sirāpa

Tt

table

টেবিল   tebil

tall

লম্বা   lamba

tank

ট্যাঙ্ক   tyank

taxi

ট্যাক্সি   tyaksi

tea

চা   cha

teacher

শিক্ষক   siksak

teeth

দাঁত   dant

telephone

টেলিফোন   teliphon

television

টিভি   tibhi

ten

১০   das

দশ

tennis

টেনিস   tenis

tent

তাঁবু   tambu

thief

চোর   chor

thread

সুতা   suta

three

তিন   tin

throat

গলা   gala

thumb

অঙ্গুষ্ঠ   angusth

ticket

টিকিট   tikit

tiger

বাঘ   bagh

toe

পদাঙ্গুলি   padanguli

a b c d e f g h i j J k l m n o p q r s **t** u v w x y z

Left sidebar

a b c d e f g h i j k l m n o p q r s **t** u v w x y z

tofu
টফু — taphu

tomato
টম্যাটো — tameto

tongue
জিভ — jiv

tool
টুল — tul

toothbrush
টুথ ব্রাশ — tuthabras

toothpaste
দাঁতের মাজন — danter majan

tortoise
কচ্ছপ — kacchap

towel
তোয়ালে — toaley

tower
মিনার — minar

toy
খেলনা — khelna

tractor
ট্র্যাক্টর — tryaktar

train
রেল গাড়ী — relgari

tree

বৃক্ষ   briksa

triangle

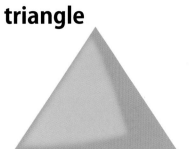

ত্রিভুজ   tribhuj

tub

টব   tab

tunnel

সুড়ঙ্গ   suranga

turnip

শালগম   salgam

tyre
US English **tire**

চাকা   chaka

Uu

umbrella

ছাতা   chata

uncle

কাকা   kaka

uniform

অভিন্ন পোশাক
abhinna poshak

university

বিশ্ববিদ্যালয়
bisbabidyala

utensil

বাসনপত্র   basanpatra

Vv

vacuum cleaner

ভ্যাকুয়াম ক্লীনার
bhyakuyam klinar

valley

উপত্যকা   upatyaka

van

ভ্যান   vain

vase

দানি   dani

vault

সিন্দুক   sinduk

vegetable

শাকসব্জি   saksabji

veil

পর্দা   parda

vet

পশুচিকিৎসক
pasuchikitsak

village

গ্রাম   gram

violet

বেগুনী   beguni

violin

বেহালা   behala

volcano

আগ্নেয়গিরি
agneyagiri

volleyball

ভলিবল খেলা
bhalibal khela

vulture

শকুনি   sakuni

Ww

waist

কোমর   komar

waitress

ওয়েট্রেস   oyetres

wall

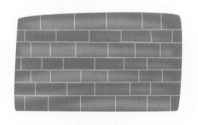

প্রাচীর   prachir

wallet

মানিব্যাগ   manibyag

walnut

আখরোট   akhrot

wand

কর্তৃত্বের প্রতীকস্বরূপ বাহিত দণ্ড
kartriter pratiksarup bahait danda

wardrobe

পোশাকের আলমারী
posaker almari

warehouse

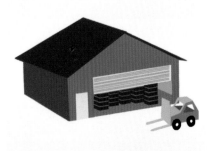

গুদাম   gudam

wasp

বোলতা   bolta

watch

ঘড়ি   ghari

water

জল   jal

watermelon

তরমুজ   taramuj

web

জাল   jaal

whale

তিমি মাছ   timi

wheat

গম   gam

wheel

চাকা   chaka

whistle

বাঁশি   banshi

white

সাদা   sada

wife

স্ত্রী   stri

window

জানলা   janala